Frederick William Faber

The 'Civiltà cattolica' on Father Faber's Spiritual Works

Frederick William Faber

The 'Civiltà cattolica' on Father Faber's Spiritual Works

ISBN/EAN: 9783337201715

Printed in Europe, USA, Canada, Australia, Japan

Cover: Foto ©Lupo / pixelio.de

More available books at **www.hansebooks.com**

THE 'CIVILTÀ CATTOLICA'

ON

FATHER FABER'S SPIRITUAL WORKS.

𝔗ranslated, b𝔶 permission,

FROM THE NUMBERS FOR AUGUST 3 AND 17.

———

LONDON: BURNS AND OATES,

Portman Street and Paternoster Row.

1872.

It is hardly necessary to say that the *Civiltà Cattolica* is the most authoritative organ of the illustrious Society of Jesus.

The Author of this article, besides giving his kind permission for its publication in English, has made a few additions to it for this Translation.

THE 'CIVILTÀ CATTOLICA'

FATHER FABER'S SPIRITUAL WORKS.

I.

As certain of Father Faber's volumes appeared in Italian, a short eulogium of each was published in the *Civiltà Cattolica*; but now that the full version of his spiritual works is before us, we propose to speak of them to our readers at greater length. To do so fitly is more difficult than appears at first sight. The books are so well known that an analytical review would be out of place, as would the selection of specimen passages; nor would there be any advantage in giving a *résumé* or a critique of them, as those of our readers who are interested in spiritual works have already formed a favourable judgment concerning them. However, a periodical may be the echo of public opinion, when it is not the voice which forms it; and then nothing pleases its readers so much, or binds them to it with so close a tie, as to find in its pages the expression of their own view. We desire nothing better for our article than that it should not merely repeat, but harmonise the many words of praise in which the connoisseurs of ascetical writings have spoken of the great merit of these volumes.

There is a maxim of St. Alphonso which will help to give a certain unity of thought to what we are about to say. If we remember right, he said that he liked those preachers whose words did not pass directly from the head to the tongue, but descended first into the heart, to be enkindled by its fire before rising again to the lips. This is true also of spiritual writers ; and it appears to us that all the merits of Father Faber's works may be summed up in this, that his beautiful language only came to his pen after being conceived by a noble mind, and inflamed by a still more noble heart. Many and remarkable were Father Faber's gifts in mind, and heart, and speech ; but what is more than all is their wonderful union and harmony, rarely found in so high a degree in spiritual works. Some ascetical writers of note (of such only are we speaking) are full of high thoughts, but turn out cold and dry; others are hearty and touching, but too much beneath persons of education; and very often where the thoughts are sound and full of warmth, the ornament, elegance, and charm of language is altogether wanting : but it is safe to say of each of Father Faber's volumes, that it is a literary as well as a spiritual work—the work of a great mind, and a great heart, and a great writer ; a work fashioned with consummate art by nature as well as by grace, which beautifies and enlivens the excellences of nature. This, in a word, is our panegyric, or rather the concentration, as in an

echo, of all the praises of Father Faber's spiritual
works. If we succeed in enlarging upon this idea,
besides the pleasure we shall give our readers, both
those who know these works already, and those who
are not yet sufficiently acquainted with them, we
shall satisfy an old desire of our own to give in our
pages, after the completion of the Italian version of
Father Faber's writings, a more striking demonstra-
tion of the high esteem, and, indeed, of the love which
we had for the author during his life, and which, as
he seems to live on and to speak by his works, we feel
for him still. 'Defunctus adhuc loquitur.'*

II.

Let us begin with the mental excellences of
Father Faber. We need not stay to speak of his
penetrating genius, its clearness, exquisite culture,
and originality of idea and form, because we wish to
put forward only the one thing which is the greatest
intellectual excellence of his works, namely, the *science
of faith.* He felt keenly that, as faith is the foundation of the spiritual life, so the foundation of all
spiritual theology, that is, of all ascetic science, is
the science of faith—dogmatic, positive, scholastic
theology; and that to write stable and substantial
ascetical works, a foundation must be laid of dogma,
and that well understood; in other words, the science
of theology; though, as a foundation should, it be
rather felt than seen to support affective devotion,
which, in its turn, rests firmly and safely upon the
truths of faith.

* Heb. xi. 4.

Father Faber's works are eminently spiritual because eminently theological; they speak directly to the heart, and speak efficaciously because illuminated to the full by the science of theology; they enkindle devotion because they elucidate faith; and we may say of his writings what he himself wrote of sermons: 'Let us only preach and teach the Divinity of Jesus, no matter how uninviting may be the notion of theological sermons, and we shall soon see how hearts will melt without eloquence of ours, and how Bethlehem and Calvary will give out their rich depths of tenderness to the poorest and the simplest of Christ's humble poor. To how many has meditation become quite a different thing, when they carried to the Crib or the Cross the light of our dear Lord's Divinity along with them!'*

And this light, what has Father Faber done but bring it? In his first work, *All for Jesus*, the very title of which tells that he speaks to the heart and speaks of love, how is it that he speaks so well, but by the power of that light which is full of intelligence and love? In his *Bethlehem*, what does he but bring that light to that Crib? And in his *Blessed Sacrament*, *Precious Blood*, and *Foot of the Cross*, whence that abundance of piety, devotion, and love, but from the same light? Again, the devotion to Mary, which breathes so tenderly and sublimely through his pages, is there because he ever presents to us the light of the Divine Maternity. His devotion to her is profoundly dogmatic, thoroughly grounded on the great thought of the Divine Maternity and the Incarnation of the Word; and

* *All for Jesus*, chap. vii. sect. v.

just because it is so dogmatic, it enkindles a divine
fire in the heart, at the same time that it elevates the
understanding. The very love of Mary as our Mother
becomes a thousandfold stronger and more tender
when we consider that she is our Mother because
she is the Mother of Jesus. Father Faber never
separates Mary from Jesus, or Jesus from Mary; and
his sublime and touching words concerning Mary are
touching, and tender, and devout, just because they
are theological, because he always considers the mysteries of Mary as an integral part of the sublime and
touching theology of the Incarnation.

Father Faber perceived that, in our age of intellectual culture, devotion and piety would gain im-
mensely by being nourished on a larger measure of
theological knowledge; and therefore, as he said in
the preface to the *Blessed Sacrament*, whilst others
strove to popularise the conclusions of astronomy,
geology, and other physical sciences, he endeavoured to familiarise the minds and hearts of the faithful with certain parts of the science of theology.
To this end he added to his own favourite study of
ascetical theology that of scholastic, not out of intellectual curiosity, but as the food of devotion in himself and others; so that he seems to have studied
and meditated with the heart as well as the mind,
and his study of theology was itself prayer. Thus
he was able to write both spirituality and theology
with accuracy and depth, not with the dry and ab-
struse phraseology of the schools, but rather with the
popular style and unction of one who would give in
the form of milk to little ones, the substantial nour-
ishment of the *science of faith*.

It is true that Father Faber's science was a gift of grace, as well as the fruit of genius and study. A special gift of grace indeed is that almost vision of invisible things, that sense of the supernatural which truly may be called the *science of faith*, by which a man not only feels, but speaks and writes for others of divine things with so much clearness, assurance, and life-like fidelity, that it seems rather knowledge than faith. Perhaps more than any other is this gift conspicuous in Father Faber's works. He walks at his ease and treads firmly and freely in the invisible world, penetrating the hidden things of doctrines and mysteries, of the operation of grace and sacraments, of the secrets of the world to come; he writes and describes and paints for us with such minute accuracy, such natural facility and simple familiarity, that he seems to be treating of things which may be seen even here by human eyes, and touched by human hands; or, to avail ourselves of his own words: 'As if it were the banks of the Rhine, or the olive-yards of Provence, the campagna of Rome, or the crescent shores of Naples; some place which they have seen in their travels, and whose geographical features are ever in their memory as vividly as if before their eyes.'*

III.

The special gift of God which is manifest in Father Faber's doctrinal writings appears also in his treatment of spiritual subjects. He undoubtedly studied mystical theology with the utmost care in the asceti-

---

* *All for Jesus*, chap. ix. sect. vi.

cal works of every nation, age, and school; and he
loved to read the lives of the Saints, speaking as they
do with the incomparable eloquence of example. To
great experience of the secrets of the spiritual life,
both in himself and others, he added that profound
knowledge of the human heart which is abundantly
shown in his *Conferences, Foot of the Cross,* and *Growth
in Holiness;* but all this science of theology and
philosophy, of theory and practice, would not have
sufficed for such writings as his, without that addi-
tional gift which is deservedly called the science of
Saints.

It is indeed marvellous to note the ease with which
he moves in the invisible world of grace, as if it were
the tangible world of nature, and makes us realise
the value of the least interior act of the love of God,
each of which, as he remarks, 'is a more finished
thing than a statue of Phidias or Praxiteles. It is
more firm than the foundations of the Alps. It is
more enduring than the round world, which God has
made so firm.'*

Wonderful as he is when he dwells on the secrets
of God's hidden ways with His Saints, he is more wonderful still when he displays the abundance of grace
and merit to be found in the commonest life, through
the graces ordinarily enjoyed by the faithful in the
Church of God, which result in the formation within
His Kingdom of that most numerous 'middle class,'
as Father Faber happily terms it, of pious and devout
persons, fruitful in virtue alike in the cloister and in
the world. To such does he speak in the preface
to *All for Jesus:* 'As a son of St. Philip I have es-

* *All for Jesus,* chap. viii. sect. iii.

pecially to do with the world, and with people living in the world and trying to be good there, and to sanctify themselves in ordinary vocations.'

Father Faber certainly appears, like his own St. Philip Neri or St. Francis of Sales, to be the special apostle of piety and devout life in the world, particularly to persons of highly cultivated mind. Not that his books do not suit religious and ecclesiastics, but that they do not, as so many spiritual works, apply exclusively or primarily to them. It would occupy too much of our space to quote even from memory all that is specially adapted to persons living in the world. According to him, devout life in the world ought to differ from that in religion, not merely in *degree*, but in *kind*. A Christian family should not be modelled on a religious community, as though it were a convent of lax observance. The place which obedience holds in the religious life is taken by patience in the domestic life of seculars; and what choir, and prayer, and other practices of the contemplative life are to religious, the exercise of works of charity and mercy is to persons living in the world. Thus the tainted atmosphere during a visit to a hospital will produce most readily certain flowers of virtue, and shield them most effectually from the spirit of the world. Now he speaks to religious opportune words which concern themselves and their little world alone, and again he points out what is best for those living in the great world of fashion; he would not, for instance, speak of detachment from sensible consolations to a lady whose heart was in the appearance of her horses and carriage, as he would to a Carmelite novice.

To all he shows in the distance the highest summits and the most thorny paths; but meanwhile he takes persons in the world by the hand, and leads them by the 'easy ways of Divine Love.' By showing how much can be done in every state for the glory of God, the good of souls, and the interests of Jesus—the three points on which he insists from the beginning of his first work, *All for Jesus*—he allures many souls living in the world to the spiritual life, and while keeping them humble and contented in their position with their present grace, he encourages them to higher aspirations. At one time his graceful and good-humoured satire castigates the faults, delusions, and, above all, the inconsistencies of devout persons in the world, till they smile at them themselves; and at another he pricks, and humbles, and raises up, and consoles, and comforts them, always urging them to love, and further, to love suffering and mortification as a matter of course, and without attempting to gild over their names.

We have been speaking from memory,—for to verify and quote all the passages we remember would take us too long. We will only instance that chapter of the *Creator and the Creature* entitled 'The World,' and we do so for two reasons; first, because we find in it the two different pictures of the world, drawn by different spiritual schools; one painted in the dark colours of night, the other in the brighter tints of day; and secondly, because while revealing his prudence in the direction of souls, it shows plainly the opposition between Father Faber's spirit and that of the world. His words have especial value, because such a spirit of opposition to the world is a necessity for those who seek to live in it without being of it.

Neither in speaking nor in writing did he ever condescend to modification or concession, to reticence or reserve, so often suggested by the false zeal of human spirituality as a necessary tribute to the taste of the age, and yet so powerless to draw a soul to God. No, as in doctrinal matters he never pronounced or withheld one word in order to suit the dominant spirit of Protestantism in England, so neither, to accommodate himself to the spirit of the world, did he ever pronounce or withhold one spiritual maxim. His prudence was the utterance of the whole truth; and in this lay the secret of his power to convert heretics and worldly people, as well as to direct souls to perfection, whether in the heart of the world or in the cloister.

In addition to this straightforward and sound direction, so suitable to persons living in the world, we find in Father Faber's works that high spirituality which comes from the supernatural element which is their life; his spirit is never in the least worldly, precisely because it is always supernatural. He never seems to breathe the low heavy air of the world, but remains in the high, pure, and supernatural atmosphere of the Catholic Church, with its graces, sacraments, and mysteries. This high spirituality, so full of the supernatural, is to be found in all his volumes, and shows how full his mind was of God; so that it seems to us that, if the existence of the theological virtues in a heroic degree in any author could be proved from his writings, Father Faber's works would give abundant proofs of it. The natural and moral virtues themselves are raised to a high supernatural order as the handmaids and ministers of love; and as St. Alphonso, the doctor of popular spirituality no less than of moral theology, collected all the exercises of Christian virtue in his *Practice of the Love of Jesus Christ*, so does Father Faber in his *All for Jesus*. All is ' per Ipsum, cum Ipso, et in Ipso ;' the whole spiritual life is summed up in the words of the Apostle, 'to me to live is Christ.' All spiritual science, whether speculative or practical, is reduced to the knowledge and love of God. The very knowledge of self is deepened in devout souls by its being rather the reflection of God's light than the direct result of over-much self-inspection, and by the supernatural illumination it receives from the knowledge of God, according to the maxim : ' Noverim Te, noverim me, ut amem Te, et despiciam me.' To use the striking expression of the Bishop of Birmingham, Mgr. Ullathorne, in his letter of congratulation to Father Faber on the publication of *All for Jesus:* 'It was wanted to draw "pious" people out of themselves, to tear their souls away with affectionate violence from that glutinous adhesion to their subjective, narrowed-in, and merely personal estimation of divine things and of divine ways. . . . . . It draws forth the soul out of that obscure cavern of self-complacency almost irresistibly, to place her on the side of God and of His divine interests.'*

That knowledge of God which is in the highest degree the science of faith gives to Father Faber's works the spiritual, unworldly, and supernatural character which is their greatest intellectual excellence, both as being so contrary to the spirit of this material,

* *Life and Letters of F. W. Faber*, p. 395.

human, and naturalistic age, and so conformable to the needs and legitimate tendencies of a generation by which intellectual culture is highly valued. Thanks to this excellence, not less than to their sweet affectionate unction, or their graceful and eloquent language, the success and popularity of these works has been far greater than any spiritual book could have been expected to obtain in such an age as this. The Abbot of Solesmes, in a short panegyric of Father Faber's life and works, published in the *Monde* in January 1864, says of his writings, ' Ils sont venus en leur temps ;' and he looks upon their publication in our time as a providential event. Some directors have thought it prudent not to recommend Father Faber's volumes much, lest persons who read works of so much genius, devotion, and originality, should lose their taste for the older spiritual writers, who, if less ornate and brilliant, are solid and safe in forming the spirit. Unquestionably Father Faber never intended to put forward his books to the exclusion of the standard works on the spiritual life which were his own study, and of which he industriously promoted the circulation ; but while recommending the great works of former days, he endeavoured to adapt all to the present time by saying 'non nova, sed novè.'

We may here note the gift of Divine Providence, which is ever bestowing on the Catholic Church not only new saints, but, so to speak, new types of holiness, new religious orders, congregations, and institutions, according to the fresh needs of each age; and which raises up in their proper time and place new writers of theological and spiritual books, not indeed to supplant or depose from their place of honour the classical works of every language and country which enrich the Church, but to increase more and more the treasure of mystical and ascetical theology which forms the immense Catholic library, from which the ever-living and fruitful Church draws things new and old. Among the illustrious works which are written for, but will outlive, the present age, Father Faber's writings have an undoubted place. Whether he points out the easy ways of Divine Love in *All for Jesus*, or discloses its wonders in the *Creator and the Creature;* whether he discourses of the high mysteries of faith, hope, and charity in *Bethlehem*, the *Precious Blood*, and the *Blessed Sacrament;* teaches the noblest spiritual science, that of suffering for Jesus, in the *Foot of the Cross;* enters into the minutest particulars of the spiritual life in the *Conferences*, or rises to the scientific explanation of its general principles in *Growth in Holiness*, he always stands forth as a great spiritual master, endowed by God with that science of the Saints, practical as well as speculative, which is the highest art of all, ' ars artium regimen animarum.' Above all, in that work of his which is professedly a manual of spirituality, *Growth in Holiness*, it was his aim to translate, so to speak, the ancient spiritual teaching into modern thought and language ; and he tells us concerning it what he says also about theology in the *Blessed Sacrament.* He endeavoured to familiarise the minds and hearts of the faithful with both the one and the other; and with both alike did he succeed, thanks to that light of the *science of faith*, which inflames the heart as well as enlightens the understanding. Thus from the mental excellences, which shine conspicuously in Father Faber's works, we pass naturally to those of his heart.

IV.

Father Faber possesses that divine science which nourishes and gives life to the affections, rather than renders them dry and barren; which passes from the mind to the heart, where dogma and spiritual teaching are transformed into devotion and love. To him the sublime doctrines of the Divine Perfections, and of the three Divine Persons, Father, Son, and Holy Ghost, are devotion and love; devotion and love again are the doctrines of the Incarnate Word, of the Virgin Mother, of the Sacraments, and above all of the great Sacrament of faith and love. In the same way the teachings of theology concerning the Pope and the Church become devotion and love to the Pope and the Church; in fact, all knowledge of God, all science of the Saints and of the spiritual life, is for Father Faber's beautiful soul a holy passion. To put the whole into one word, all is love; hence the sweet and powerful attractiveness of all his works. What else is the meaning of the title of his first book, *All for Jesus?* He says himself that 'All for Jesus' is the same thing as 'All for love.'* 'The name of his first book,' remarked Mgr. Manning very truly, 'is like a note in music; in all his writings, in all his teachings, there is the same strain throughout—All for Jesus.'† We find the same idea in the *Dublin Review* for January 1864: 'This may be said to be the key-note of all that followed. They are one and

---

* *All for Jesus*, chap. viii. sect. iy.
† *Life and Letters of F. W. Faber*, p. 519

all as harmonies elaborated out of this octave; the first few simple notes giving forth a flood of sound, rich, intricate, and sweet.' But more than this, Father Faber's life—as the writer of it, Father Bowden, has happily said—may be summed up in the simple words: He served Jesus out of love. Yes, his life was 'All for Jesus,' and therefore he could write as he did; as its history, so his spiritual works may be summed up in the same formula: To serve God out of love. To him love, but love never separated from holy and salutary fear, was the beginning of the spiritual life, its progress and perfection, its first and last word. From the first fundamental truth of religion and of the whole spiritual life, that God is our first Beginning and our last End, the one great consequence which he draws, and in which all else is contained and expressed, is *love*—to serve God out of love. To this refer the two magnificent chapters of the *Creator and the Creature*, in which he asks, 'What it is to be a creature?' 'What it is to have a Creator?' and answers in substance that the creature, as being all of God and for God, can only correspond to the creative love of the Creator by a service which is all of love. After these chapters, so simple and yet so deep, so full of instruction and devotion, come five others which abound in light and fire: 'Why does God wish us to love Him?' 'Why does God love us?' 'Our means of loving God;' 'Our actual love of God;' 'In what way God repays our love.' We may rightly say that the *Creator and the Creature* stands in relation to Father Faber's other works as their elementary philosophy, and contains his whole spirit in its speculative, as *All for Jesus* does in its practical form; both the one and the other breathing alike what is the spirit of all, the service of God out of love—a personal love, arising especially from the intimate conviction that God loves each one personally with the unspeakable love of Creation and Redemption; so that this spirit of love is, as it were, a spark from the exceeding love of the Heart of God the Creator, and of the Sacred Heart of Jesus the Redeemer.

This spirit of Father Faber's heart, which appears in all his works, is precisely that of the beautiful heart of St. Philip, a spirit of love: not merely a sentimental love of barren affection and heated imagination, but a love which understood to the full the greatness of God and the nothingness of the creature; a filial love, which dutifully feels that 'Nemo tam Pater quasi Deus,' and which to the most intimate familiarity unites the deepest humility and reverence; a love full of faith and full of hope, that virtue which seems at certain times in the spiritual life more difficult of attainment than faith or love; and thus a love which, feeling the weakness of its own powers, is full of courageous confidence in God, and so avoids that dispiriting cowardice which is the most fatal impediment to spiritual progress; a love which destroys the love of the world, of self, and of aught else but God; a penitent love, always united to that abiding sorrow of compunction, to which he gives the sweet name of *pardoned love;* a noble and generous love, which is not satisfied with small things, which gives little things with a large heart, and great things as counting them nothing, which is ever aspiring to perfection, disdaining all unworthy aims, and every sort of reserve or compromise with God, which never calculates in order to give the least that duty requires, but would rather give the more that it can than the less that it ought; a love which looks on piety and a devout life not as a burden, but as grace and happiness; a love to which sacrifices are dear; a love at one time held in holy captivity, at another set free by a holy liberty of spirit, but at all times full of joy; in short, a spirit of love which possesses in itself the true secret of making virtue and piety and Christian holiness popular, that is, to make them *loveable*. Thus did Father Faber inherit the spirit of his dear Father St. Philip Neri, and continue that school which was called the school of Christian mirth, just because it was a school of love. Of the fulness of love he speaks its language, speaks from the heart and to the heart, in the language which becomes him so well, the language of reason and faith. Well he knew that true love does not spring from the *ignis fatuus* of eloquence or the excitement of fancy, but must be enkindled and illuminated by intelligence and faith. In a word, this spirit of intelligent love, which is the life of all his works, reflects and concentrates for us, as in a glass, the excellences of Father Faber's wonderful mind and still more wonderful heart.

V.

With such a mind and heart as Father Faber's it needs no art or study to be eloquent; but he had made language his art and study, and was in addition a born poet as well as an orator, so that his eloquence is also poetry. When the poet Wordsworth heard that young Faber was about to undertake the cure of souls, he said that England was losing a poet; but we should rather say that Catholic England gained a poet, not only by his beautiful hymns, which are most popular in so many schools and churches, but because his spiritual works, though written in prose, have in them all the beauty, fire, and life of Christian poetry. He intended to sacrifice poetry to religion; but instead of that, religion gave life, nobility, and a divine character to his poetical genius. Those high natural qualities of the soul of a poet,—creative power, a love of beauty, a taste for grandeur, a clear-sighted mind, an ardent heart, a lively imagination and exquisite perception, richness of language, picturesqueness of style, and all the other qualifications which go to the making of a poet,—found in the realities of the spiritual world no less poetical a field than the fair world of fancy which the poet loves to create. If, then, England lost a poet of nature, that loss was a gain to Faber himself, and a double gain, we may say, to spirituality; first, because the spiritual life, from the essentially prosaic character of its daily practice, is a great gainer by those attractions of poetry which make it more loveable, and so more popular; and, secondly, because the poverty of our spiritual library is enriched by these beautiful volumes, which are a *chef-d'œuvre* of spirituality, and in the original, if not in the translation, of literature as well, and which are fitted both by nature and art to present us with the picturesque and poetical appearance of a spiritual landscape-garden. Nature had made him a poet, and grace, in sanctifying him, sanctified this its beautiful gift.

In truth, to speak of poetry alone, religion appears

to have a tendency to enkindle the poetical spark in
holy souls to whom it has been denied by nature; so
that we generally find in the words of Saints about
divine things a spontaneous and picturesque language,
which is really the poetical element of that style which
an illustrious writer, speaking of the holy Curé of
Ars, calls the style of the Saints.* He is certainly
right in saying that the Saints, with all their variety,
have a style of writing peculiar to themselves, in
which they speak of God, of man, and of his nature,
with so much unction, freedom, and beauty, that it
reads to us as poetry. This is especially true of Father Faber's style, which in truth is not only the style
of the Saints, inasmuch as, being the style of grace, it
differs from the style of nature, but is also the happy
union of nature, art, and grace, in which we see at
once the theologian and the philosopher, the spiritual
man and the orator, the painter and the poet. In
fact, we see in it the whole man, so that we find sin-
gularly verified the bold saying of Boileau, the 'style'
is the man,' or rather what Cicero said with greater
moderation and truth, 'Oratio vultus animi est.' His
words come full of life from mind and heart, and thus
come as the living image of the man to his mouth and
to his pen—'tel sur le papier qu'à la bouche,' according to Montaigne's rule of eloquence—he wrote as
he spoke, and spoke as he thought and felt. This is
more than commonly true of Father Faber, inasmuch
as his written words were first preached in his familiar
discourses at the Oratory; so that we may literally
apply to his works the saying of St. Alphonso which
we quoted at the outset, that the language of the sacred

* Léon Gautier, 'Le Monde,' April 9, 1864.

orator is matured in his mind, and inflamed in his heart before coming to his mouth. It is then committed to paper, that he may preach not only in fugitive words to a limited audience, but unchangeably to thousands and thousands of souls.

VI.

Those who study Father Faber's works will find in them no traces of what is called the midnight oil. His beautiful pages flow on in a stream of natural eloquence, and read like a poetical improvisation. The truth is, that he wrote like one inspired, for many hours at once, without pause or erasure, and as if without fatigue; but the real work of his books was done, to use his own expression, in the long periods of their *gestation*. For whole months he read and studied, meditated and prayed; and with mind and heart thus charged, he first put on paper well-arranged notes for his ordinary sermons in the Oratory. In his case preaching was, as the *Dublin Review* for January 1864 well puts it, not an effort, but a relief; it was the outpouring of the abundance of mind and heart; for to speak of divine and spiritual things was no less a pleasure to himself than to the audience who hung upon his words. After his sermons, he often added to his notes the changes and improvements which the fervour of preaching had suggested to him; and these papers, together with others prepared with order and care as the outline of each treatise, after being laid by for a considerable time, frequently long enough to satisfy the precept of Horace, 'nonum in annum,' were reconsidered and matured until they furnished the necessary matter for his books, which were then written as easily as casts are taken from a mould. All the eight volumes were written and published in the short space of eight years, between January 1853 and December 1860, notwithstanding numerous other occupations and continued ill health. The following particulars are taken from the history of his life.[*]

On the 16th of January 1853, after High Mass on the Feast of the Holy Name of Jesus, he began to write the first of his spiritual works, *All for Jesus;* the first in order of time, and in reputation, if not in merit. It was the first-fruits of his preaching in the beginnings of the Oratory, and he tells the frequenters of that church, in its affectionate dedication to them, that they will find in his book many things which they have often heard him say in the pulpit. The first edition, though a large one, was exhausted in a month; a second, third, and fourth, numbering together thousands of copies, followed rapidly; and now who can reckon the editions and translations of *All for Jesus?*[†] This happy result was due to several causes; but from the first, Father Faber's humble and joyful heart would only recognise one, the subject he had chosen—*All for Jesus;* 'my subject was my success.'

Growth in Holiness was published towards the end of 1854. More than an orator, it shows Father Faber as a spiritual father and great master of the direction of souls; and the whole book displays the discretion, mature judgment, and counsel of private spiritual

[*] *Life and Letters of F. W. Faber,* chaps. xi. and xii.
[†] In 1869 there had been published 100,000 copies of *All for Jesus,* in seven languages. *Trans.*

advice, rather than the eloquence of the pulpit. He had planned three books, in order to comprehend the whole spiritual life; the first was to have been *First Fervours*, and the last the *Gate of Heaven:* unfortunately we only have the one which was to hold the middle place, but even by itself it is a treasure.

Father Faber chose the Feast of Corpus Domini in 1855 for the publication of his work on the Blessed Sacrament, which was based upon a course of sermons preached during the octave of that feast in the preceding year. It is divided into four books, in which the august mystery of Jesus veiled is treated as the greatest work of God, the great devotion of Catholics, and the picture and representation of the mysteries and hidden ways of God, and of the Incarnate Word.

The *Creator and the Creature*, of which the author says that it stands to his other works in the relation of source and origin, was published towards the end of 1856. In it he discloses the wonders of divine love, and especially his own habitual method of regarding the things of God and of the spiritual life. This he had studied and meditated for years, so that in his preface, while submitting as usual every word to the judgment of the Church, he could express the hope that every private critic (and such even Father Faber had) would be as slow and careful to judge as he had been to write. To us this work appears his *chef-d'œuvre.*

Before the Lent of 1858 he brought out the *Foot of the Cross, or the Dolours of Mary.* It had been sketched out as far back as 1847, and written fully in 1855, as it was intended to accompany a projected work on the Passion of our Divine Redeemer, entitled

Calvary. Of course, while treating of the compassion of Mary, he is naturally led to speak a good deal of the Passion of Jesus. We need not say that the subjects of these books were frequently dealt with in his sermons; his Lenten course in 1857 was on Calvary; and that of May on Bethlehem, his last work, as we shall presently see.

The volume of *Spiritual Conferences*, published early in 1859, represents more than his other books the form of the sermons which he was in the habit of preaching in the Oratory. M. Louis Veuillot, in his *Historiettes et Fantaisies*, calls it 'livre ascétique, livre anglais, livre traduit;' and yet he is charmed with it, and says, 'véritablement le docteur Faber est un maître homme.' Then, remarking how practically it touches the roots and fibres of the heart, he adds in his playful way, 'ce P. Faber est un maître écorcheur, et il a des pinces étranges pour saisir les fibres les plus ténues et les plus cachées sous la peau qu'il enlève dextrement.'

The *Precious Blood* was published in Lent 1860, and dedicated to the Confraternity of that name at the Oratory, which at that time numbered thirty thousand members, a number which since then has been largely increased. This shows how popular devotion to the Precious Blood is in England, and Father Faber could again say, ' My subject is my success.'

The last of his great spiritual works, *Bethlehem*, appeared at the beginning of Advent in the same year, and contains the mysteries of the Incarnation and of the Sacred Infancy, treated as might be expected from such a mind and heart and pen as Father

Faber's. He used to say that he wrote the rest of his books to please others, but *Bethlehem* to please himself.

We have spoken only of those spiritual works which have been translated into Italian; but Father Faber wrote others, both in poetry and prose. Some were begun or merely sketched out, and may be found in the *Notes on Doctrinal and Spiritual Subjects*, published in two volumes after his death, which took place on the 26th of September 1863. He was rather more than forty-nine years old, having been born on the 14th of June 1814; and eighteen years had not elapsed since, on the 17th of November 1845, he had left Anglicanism to enter the Catholic Church. Had he lived longer, he might have written more; but what he has written is so much and so valuable, that we may well console ourselves with the thought, that before his death he was enabled to pour forth in writing his beautiful soul almost to the full, and thus, as it were, to conclude that hymn to the glory of God which was contained within him, according to the prayer,

> ' Avant que de mes jours s'approche le terme,
> Que je puisse épuiser l'hymne que je renferme !'

VII.

Our best thanks are due to Canon Theologian Mussa, who has given to Italy the translation of this beautiful hymn of Father Faber's mind and heart and pen; and also to Cavaliere Marietti, who has added this to the many Catholic publications for which he is distinguished. Since the translation of the first was published, Father Faber's works have been as successful in Italy as in England, America, and the other countries where they have been published. The venerable Abbot of Solesmes, Dom Guéranger, said happily, in the panegyric of Father Faber's life and works which we have already quoted, that such spiritual writings are each in their own age a benefit to Catholic souls, and a gift of the Holy Spirit to the Church; and that since the *Devout Life of St. Francis of Sales*, it would be difficult to find other works like his. Again, an American review, the *Catholic World* of New York, says with truth, that Father Faber is the most popular spiritual writer of the age.

His works were an especial gift of God to England; but they are also a gift to the spiritual literature of the Catholic world. For England they were a gift exactly suited to the time of that great Catholic movement or revival, which Dr. Newman, in his sermon before the first Provincial Council of Westminster, so justly styled the second spring of England; a spring in which—we may say it without injury to any one—next to Cardinal Wiseman and his worthy successor Mgr. Manning, no one had more share than Dr. Newman himself and Father Faber. To speak, however, only of the latter, his spiritual works were undoubtedly the fairest flowers of this second spring, flowers which have diffused the sweet perfume of Christ throughout the Catholic world. It may be that some native beauties are lost by translation, and that what was pleasing in the original is not so in its new dress,—for each country has tastes of its own; but still, a book of Father Faber's, although 'livre ascétique, livre anglais, livre traduit,' always pleases everybody, and the 'pourtant

j'y prends goût' of M. Veuillot may be said by all
who have good taste, or, better still, Catholic taste.
Father Faber is a Catholic, rather than an English, author, and especially Catholic because especially
Roman; 'very, very Roman,' as he felt himself be-
coming even before he was a Catholic. The fundamental cause of his great success in promoting the
spiritual life in England, and the chief of the excellences of Father Faber's mind and heart and pen on
which we have dilated, is that mind and heart and
pen were all *Roman.* We believe that to his beautiful soul this praise would have been more grateful
than any other; it alone would have sufficed him;
and with it we will conclude.

The ideal of a sacred orator and a spiritual writer,
which we took from a saying of St. Alphonso Liguori,
is fulfilled by Father Faber in a high degree. His
words are conceived in a mind enlightened by great
genius and lively faith, inflamed in a heart full of
tenderness and love, and thus, filled with life and
heat and beauty, they come forth from his lips as
shining darts of fire to illuminate minds and enkindle
hearts. Science, poetry, and love; truth, goodness,
and beauty; instruction, persuasion, and delight;
what is useful as well as what is pleasant, nature and
grace,—we find all in high degree and sweet harmony
in that sacred eloquence which is poured forth from
Father Faber's mind and heart to his lips and to his
pen. Thus to St. Alphonso's maxim we may join the
inspired words of the Book of Proverbs: 'Cor sapientis
erudiet os ejus: the heart of the wise shall instruct
his mouth.'*

* Chap. xvi. 23.

We have much pleasure in stating, in addition to what we have said, that when Cavaliere Marietti presented to the Holy Father Pius IX. a handsomely-bound copy of Father Faber's works, his Holiness deigned to write the following words on the letter which accompanied the offering:

'July 31, 1872.

'I highly approve of the publication in Italian of the excellent Father Faber's works. I give my blessing to the translator and the publisher, engaging the latter to continue the publication of good and sound works.—P. PP. IX.'

LONDON:
ROBSON AND SONS, PRINTERS, PANCRAS ROAD, N.W.

www.ingramcontent.com/pod-product-compliance
Lightning Source LLC
Chambersburg PA
CBHW021458090426
42739CB00009B/1782